BOOTSVILLE

Christopher M. White

Independently Published by j3eight, ltd.

First Edition

ISBN 9798642067666

Independently Published by j3eight, ltd
j3eight.com

To

MY WIFE, WHO IS INFINITELY
UNDERSTANDING.

MY CHILDREN, WHO INDULGE THEIR FATHER,
NO MATTER HOW WEIRD.

MY TEAM, WHO HAS TRUSTED ME TO LEAD
THEM THROUGH THE GOOD AND BAD.

AND TO YOU, THE READER WHO IS LOOKING
FOR A BETTER WAY -
IT IS OUT THERE.

Table of Contents

CHAPTER 1: BOOTSVILLE, STRAPSYLVANIA

It is hard not to notice the peculiar people of the city of Bootsville, located in the District of Strapsylvania.

They are hard-working, dedicated, and independent folk.

Their attitudes are pleasant enough for most, and you rarely hear them complain - not that it would make a difference if they did (or so you might hear them say).

What makes them so peculiar is their posture.

While they are about their business, they are hunched over with their hands clasping the straps of their work boots.

It is not merely a peculiar sight, but the longer you view it, the more empathetically uncomfortable you become.

But the citizens of Bootsville go about it as if they were born holding a bootstrap.

After all, they are, in fact, a hard-working, dedicated, and independent group.

For generations, they have worked this way.

They doggedly pull at their bootstraps while shuffling about their work.

Yes shuffling.

A person cannot take full steps when all hunched over.

If you ask them how they are, many will say, sardonically so, that they are "living the dream" or "busier than a one-armed wallpaper hanger."

If you ask them why they are working this way, you will more often than not be met with condescending answers.

As if you are a small child asking a ridiculous question.

"We are self-made people, and we lift ourselves up on our own."

"This is the way our father, his father, and his father's father always worked."

"I trust myself to get my work done."

Or, "I carry a significant amount of weight in my position, and you wouldn't understand the strain I am under."

To that point, they take a great deal of pride in their ability to exert significant strain and pull on their bootstraps.

Their most exceptional citizens have very well defined arm and back muscles from their extraordinary feats of pulling over the years.

You might think, from their posture, that they live a small life.

Live in small houses.

Shop in small stores.

Work in small offices.

But they don't.

Most have modest normal-sized houses.

When they are not working, they stand as any person would.

Albeit, after years of pulling, a person's posture would be irresistibly drawn forward and down.

So how did they build their city, if during their working hours they were less than half their full height?

For an outsider to Bootsville, this is one of the most disturbing sights to witness.

To reach higher, the Bootsvillians, while determinedly holding onto their bootstrap, would step on each other.

Stepping on people gave those at the upper levels a slightly higher view and the ability to work at an unremarkably higher level.

This process resulted in any project of significance taking a very long time to complete and a significant pile of Bootsvillians are needed to allow one person to reach the heights required to complete the project.

At the center of Bootsville resides a statue of a hunched-over man.

The figure portrayed in the statue is at a level that most working Bootsvillians can't see, but on it, where every Bootsvillian can see, is inscribed their primary teaching, "Lift yourself up by your bootstraps."

This hard-working, dedicated, and independent group of people found the words inspiring and, in every aspect of their work, were living out the teaching in their community.

But it is in this group that you could meet one Bootsvillian who is less than inspired.

His name is Stanley Armstrong.

CHAPTER 2: STANLEY ARMSTRONG

Stanley Armstrong is the epitome of a middle of the pile Bootsvillian.

He stands on a couple of people to get his job done, but he is also providing support for the people standing on him.

Stanley is responsible for organizing and routing supplies and tools from the ground to the top.

It is a position that is respected, and Stanley treats people below and above with respect.

But even so, Stanley is frustrated with his position.

Looking down, Stanley sees the various supplies available from the suppliers of Bootsville. Ahead, he sees the work previously completed.

But looking up... Stanley can't get a clear vision of what is needed.

Stanley's fellow Bootsvillians below him struggle to get him the supplies that he needs because they can't see where the supplies are as well as Stanley, and because they are trying to get the supplies while holding on to their bootstraps.

The Bootsvillians above him can't see the struggle below and can only understand the needs in front of them.

Thus, Stanley bears the brunt of the demand from above, without being able to see precisely what they need as he struggles to organize those below.

All the while striving to hold onto his bootstraps.

Stanley recently finds himself wondering if there isn't a better way.

And it was on one of those wondering days while Stanley was bent over his grill making supper for his family, that he saw a couple of people making their way down his street.

They didn't look like normal Bootsvillians, but at first, Stanley couldn't tell why they looked out of place.

Their clothes were familiar.

They wore standard work boots.

But there was something different about them.

As they got closer to Stanley, it struck him; they were standing tall and straight, without the slightest bit of lean, curve, or arch in their back.

Younger Bootsvillians often stood tall early in their careers, but usually, the weight of their work would start hunching them over within a year or so of starting.

These individuals were not young, but yet they walked as if they were.

As they approached, Stanley watched them, while trying not to look like he was watching them.

And as they were preparing to walk past his house, they stopped and called to him.

Stanley faced an awkward situation.

One you are familiar with if you have ever been people watching and inadvertently make eye contact with one of your subjects of observation.

At first, he made the patented move that says, "You caught me" - quickly looking down at his grill, then back up again just a quick.

They asked their question again.

"Is this the Armstrong residence?"

Now that he was fully present, Stanley was able to engage them.

"Yes," he said.

"Fantastic! We are looking for Stanley Armstrong. You must be him."

"I am. How can I help you?" Stanley quickly felt his confidence reassert itself.

"We would like to talk to you about an opportunity."

"My name is Skye Alerio," said the woman, "and this is Freeman Walker."

Stanley reached out to shake their hands and immediately notices the next peculiarity.

Bootsvillians have firm handshakes with specific callous patterns developed from grabbing their bootstraps all day long.

While these strangers' grips were firm, there were none of the standard callouses.

With his curiosity now fully stoked, he took notice of their boots.

Specifically, he took to examining their bootstraps.

Their bootstraps showed no exceptional wear and tear.

The straps looked no more worn out than their boots.

The bootstraps on most Bootsvillian boots are heavily worn, showing the wear and tear of constant pulling.

In fact, it is a reason to celebrate when a Bootsvillian has pulled so hard that their straps come off.

New Bootstrap Day is evidence of how hard they have been straining against the weight of their position.

Stanley was even hopeful that he would be able to celebrate a New Bootstrap Day sometime soon.

The bootstraps of these two did not show significant wear and tear, nor did their posture demonstrate that they were bearing up under any notable strain.

They had none of the signs of being hard-working and dedicated to pulling themselves up by their bootstraps.

Stanley started to worry that these people were not the right sort of people to have on his front porch.

He was almost sure that they weren't independent either, though he had nothing to prove it yet.

Far be it from Stanley to be rude, but he told himself he would seek a way to excuse himself as soon as possible.

Meanwhile, Skye had started talking again.

"Stanley, we are looking for a person like you."

"We've been asking people all over Bootsville for someone with organizational skills, and your name keeps coming up."

See! Stanley told himself, I knew they weren't the independent-worker type.

They've come here to try and get me to do work for them.

Sky continued.

"We would very much like to talk with you about taking a position on our team."

Freeman chimed in.

"That's right."

"Skye and I are two parts of a team that we are building, but we lack the skills needed to complete our project."

"It is a big project that we are hoping will change the lives of our community for good."

For one thing, Stanley had never heard someone say they were lacking.

It sounded like complaining and made him uneasy.

And another thing, a good Bootsvillian never says they need someone else's help.

It was becoming clear to Stanley that these people were not normal Bootsvillians.

Freeman went on.

"We know we have just dropped in on you unexpectedly, but we would very much like to meet with you formally to discuss what we are trying to accomplish and see if you would be a good fit."

A good fit, Stanley thought scoffingly, I fit just fine at my current job.

Wanting to end this increasingly uncomfortable encounter, he answered, "Uh, I don't know. Um, I am going to take food into my family, and we are about to sit down for supper and..."

Skye cut him off.

"Of course, we apologize for interrupting."

"Why don't we come to your job tomorrow, and we can talk?"

Stanley saw his opportunity; he could get out of this conversation and probably avoid them at the job site.

He knows when everyone is hunched over, only seeing what is directly below and in front of them, it is easy to hide in a crowd.

Stanley immediately made a plan to do just that.

"Sure sure," Stanley said, "now if you will excuse me."

Skye and Freeman shook his hand again, and said their goodbyes.

Stanley slipped inside a quickly as he could.

That evening he thought about the encounter.

He thought about how weird it was.

But he also thought that there was something curious and intriguing about these people.

It was every bit his intent to avoid them the next day, but there was something about them and their "project" that intrigued him.

Even if he didn't know what it was yet.

CHAPTER 3: CAN I ASK YOU A QUESTION?

The next morning Stanley made sure to remember to keep a low profile at work.

He put on his work boots, assumed the position, and shuffled off to the job site.

Nothing that day was particularly impressive and Stanley soon settled into the routine and put Skye and Freeman out of his head.

He routed requests down and tried to get the requested items up to the top until break time.

Yes, Bootsvillians take breaks, mostly to prevent piles from falling over.

Breaks were mandated after a large pile fell over onto a crowd of people resulting in no small amount of work for the Bootsvillian lawyers.

As the pile was disassembling for a break, Stanley heard his name being called.

He immediately flushed with dread.

The drone of the routine had made him forget how much he did not want to continue the conversation with these two very usual people.

Stanley hoped that he would be able to get down into the crowd and out of sight as soon as possible.

But there was a problem.

The pile was not moving very quickly, and Stanley was having trouble getting down.

He thought there was a problem with the lower levels letting people off; sometimes, the lifters didn't move very fast.

But he was wrong.

People weren't moving very quickly because they were staring at something.

Stanley had to shift carefully to see what was going on.

His surprise was equal to his dread.

Waving at him and standing at full height were Skye and Freeman.

Three things went through Stanley's mind.

One, cannot be repeated in mixed company.

Two, he would not be able to hide from them with them standing there like that.

Three, everyone else saw these two very odd individuals wanted to talk with him.

The citizens of Bootsville are not the kind to openly talk about this kind of situation, but they are also not the kind to miss a spectacle.

Stanley's best course of action was to get down and take them somewhere to talk - away from so many eyes.

On his way down, he quickly asked his higher up for some extra time, before shuffling off to meet with Skye and Freeman.

Sensing Stanley's anxieties, Skye and Freeman took Stanley to a quiet coffee shop.

Once there, they wasted no time in getting to the point.

"So," Skye started, " what is it about us that makes you so uncomfortable."

Skye had a wry smile that indicated she already knew the issues and was comfortable charging headlong into them, though she valued allowing people to come to their conclusions.

Stanley, to Skye's surprise, didn't hesitate.

She liked that.

"Well, to start with, your entire stance and appearance are different from other Bootsvillians."

"You stand at full height during the time we are all working, so the weight of your work can't be that heavy... if you carry any at all."

"It doesn't appear that you have been pulling on your bootstraps."

"I just don't know how you are getting anywhere exerting so little effort."

Stanley was direct but not rude.

He had the tone of one who was genuinely puzzled by what he was seeing.

But there was something else, that curiosity from the night before was starting to creep into his consciousness.

And Skye sensed it.

"So?" Skye asked.

Stanley looked confused.

"Why don't you ask us your question."

Skye wasn't asking him as much as she was opening the door.

Stanley found himself walking through it.

"You say you are building a team and that you need someone like me."

"You don't have the signs of hard-workers, dedicated to their jobs, and you don't appear to be very independent."

"Yet, you also say you have a project that will do good."

"How can you be successful and build something good if you aren't pulling yourself up by your bootstraps?"

"What makes you so different?"

The statements and questions flooded out of Stanley.

He realized that these people were putting him off his usual composure, but his anxiety was starting to diminish.

Freeman, for his part, sat back in his seat and relaxed.

He had been studying Stanley, wondering if Stanley could be the kind of person they needed.

This man's skills were well-spoken of, but they needed more than just skills.

They needed someone who could rise above the ways of a flawed cultural system to be a part of their team.

In seeing Stanley's curiosity and directness on display, Freeman was confident that, if Skye could work her magic, Stanley could be their guy.

And with the precision of a surgeon, Skye asked, "Stanley, can I ask you a question?"

CHAPTER 4: SKYE ALERIO

Skye Alerio was always asking questions.

Skye became discontent very early with the bootstrapping culture.

She found herself unmotivated and some days verging on depressed.

The culture of Bootsville was open to minimal questioning and was even less tolerant of anyone who went against the grain.

Their lack of tolerance for change was not overt, but rather a slow cutting off.

A kind of slow isolation that is not only perceived but real and which is hard to endure, even when you don't agree with those around you.

And for most who experienced it, the isolation caused them to abandon their aspiration and re-adopt the Bootsvillian cultural touchstones.

This reality and fear led Skye to try to "tow-the-line" for far too long.

But one day she could no longer stand feeling that she was not getting anywhere meaningful nor making a significant difference.

So, she let go of her bootstraps and stood up.

She did not know of any other Bootsvillian who had just stood up in the middle of their job without provocation.

But there she was, standing at her full height looking out over the backs of her co-workers.

It wasn't immediately evident to her co-workers what was happening.

As a whole they were not very aware of their surroundings with their faces pointed at the ground all day.

But it became evident as Skye started to laugh.

Skye was laughing at first because of the freedom she felt.

Then because of the ridiculousness of the picture of all these hunched over backs straining against their weight.

But ultimately, she laughed because she didn't know what else to do.

She just laughed long and loud.

Her laughing is what caught her co-workers' attention.

Some of those around her were shocked into silence.

Others were frustrated at her laughter.

And few were sneering at her with long sideways stares.

But for Skye, they all looked a little bit funny.

Funny and a little sad.

She stifled her laughter and made her way out of her workspace.

She didn't know where she was going, but Skye felt more free and open to possibilities than she ever had before.

That day she explored the city, just to see what there was to see.

That night she tried to explain it to her family, but they were having none of it.

They tried to explain to her that she was breaking tradition and that this was just a phase she was going through.

If she could conform and tough it out, then it would all be okay.

The problem was, Skye had never been so sure that stooping down and pulling her bootstraps was not her purpose.

She was confident her purpose was higher.

But what that purpose was wouldn't be evident to her for some time.

Unfortunately, for visionaries, sometimes the urge to leap is greater than the desire to look.

Since Skye had no one to look to or talk to about this, she very much leaped before she looked.

And there were some hard times in the days after Skye stood up.

Her family wasn't supportive.

Her community didn't provide any direction.

There were no guiding lights.
No road signs.
No burning bushes.

She was finding her way towards a vision that was not yet fully formed.
But she was determined to find it.

One day she was walking the city and just taking it all in.
As looked up at the low lying buildings and bland city streets, the first bits of inspiration started to spark in her brain.

For visionaries, sometimes a vision will manifest fully realized, without the visionary knowing where it came from.
Other times a vision will spark to life, giving just a glimpse of a picture, then it is dark again.

However a vision manifests, in that moment it is like a shot of adrenaline.

And at the moment a vision sparked to life in Skye it drove her to find the highest point in the city.

A place where she could look out on all of the rooftops.

Finding the high point wasn't hard because the tallest buildings were only several stories tall.

Piles of Bootsvillians could only stack so high before the weight on the bottom was unbearable.

She ran to the highest building and made her way to the top.

From there, she had a full view of the city.

It lay before her as a homogenous grouping of indistinct buildings.

It wasn't that attractive.

When the city's inhabitants spend most of their time bent over, they put very little care into the beauty of the things above them.

But Skye did not see a bland cityscape.

She saw a blank canvas ready to receive color.

"Is the reason no-one was reaching up was they didn't believe there was anything worth reaching up for?" Skye thought.

From her conversations with others, in the time she had stopped trying to pull herself up by her bootstraps, it was evident that they didn't believe there was any better way and that they defined success very narrowly, and stubbornly.

What if she could show them a better way?

Inspire them to reach higher.

As she stood there, the vision took shape in front of her, a canvas covered with vivid colors and shapes all animated by the wind and sun.

The excitement inside her was barely containable.

Never again would she be able to look at her city in the same way.

Unfortunately, as Skye would come to find out, the journey from vision to implementation is not an easy one.

But it became easier when she met Freeman Walker.

Chapter 5: Freeman Walker

In the time before Freeman Walker met Skye Alerio, he was the model Bootsvillian.

He excelled at his work and regularly met and exceeded quotas.

He was very well suited for his work.

He would receive supply requests and then head out to fill them.

He knew the best places to get materials and had good relationships with all of the vendors.

He was quick with a funny story but shrewd in negotiations—knowing how far he could push a vendor to maintain a great relationship and get the best deal.

The higher-ups often complimented him for his work.

Though it seemed, there was very little room for him higher up in a pile.

Despite all of his efforts and strain to pull himself higher, he was still left running the supply routes to and from the piles.

There had to be a better way.

Freeman just couldn't see it.

That is until the day he caught a glimpse of someone moving quicker than the rest of the Bootsvillians around one of his favorite vendor's shop.

He tilted his head to catch a better view.

Then he shook his head and looked again, just be sure his eyes weren't deceiving him.

Yep, he saw correctly.

That lady was standing up, trying to make an order for some supplies.

Freeman had heard rumors from some of his vendors that somebody was standing at full height, ordering odd supplies, but he paid it little mind at the time.

But now, with this person right in front of him, he was genuinely curious.

Freeman had a few moments, so he decided to head over and see what was going on.

The closer he got, the more he realized two things.

One, whoever this lady was, she had no idea how to work with vendors.

Two, Sal, the vendor, was trying his best to service everyone other than her.

Freeman knew he should be back about his route, but his curiosity was getting the better of him.

"Excuse me," Freeman said, "but you look like you need some help."

"You have no idea," said the standing lady, with no small amount of exasperation.

"I can't seem to get the vendor to pay any attention to me."

She said as both an explanation and attempt to garner some attention from the vendor.

"What's your name?" Freeman asked.

"Skye." The standing lady replied.

Freeman, one hand still on his bootstrap, reached up and said, "Well, Skye, my name is Freeman."

"Let me see what you need."

Skye, obviously thankful for the help, handed him her list.

"Well, this is an interesting list," said Freeman scanning it in thoroughly.

"I cannot say I've seen these supplies requested at the same time before."

"Nonetheless, you've come to the right vendor."

"Sal here," Freeman said half explaining and half calling out to the vendor, "is the best vendor in this section of the city."

Sal, seeing Freeman, came over obviously, and poorly, hiding his happiness to see him.

"Now Freeman, it does you no good to try and butter me up... except when it does."

He said with a smirk that turned into a laugh.

"Sal, I have a list for my friend Skye here that I need you to take a look at," Freeman said with natural confidence.

Sal took a long unsure sideways glance at Skye, but after a few seconds, he looked back at Freeman with a grin and said, "Anything for my best customer."

As Sal went about filing Freeman's order, Freeman chatted up the other regulars.

He found it useful for his job to keep on top of what was going on all over the city, and other route runners like him were the best sources of information.

Skye, for her part, just stood there somewhat perplexed.

What was happening now was far outside of her strengths.

She didn't even know that someone could have such an easy and effortless way with people.

Soon enough, Sal had gathered the supplies. "Now Freeman, your friend here has the means to pay for all this?" Sal questioned without looking at Skye.

"His friend does have the means," Skye replied.

"What's the total, Sal?" Freeman asked.

What happened next so thoroughly confounded Skye that it took some time to register what exactly had happened.

Freeman and Sal engaged in witty bartering that was at both times respectful and sharp.
Sal quoted a figure that Freeman quickly countered.
When Sal didn't move far enough, Freeman would repeat his last counter.
It appeared to Skye that Freeman had a number in mind and knew the value of what he was getting.
But he did it like it was second nature.
No guessing.
No pauses, unless they were strategic.
And no disrespect either.

This deft interchange was the first of many times that Freeman's skills in achieving an objective would benefit their relationship.
But each time was as amazing as the first to Skye.

After several minutes of bartering and bantering, Freeman got the supplies for half the amount Skye had expected to pay.
She wanted to ask how but knew she should be grateful and pay Sal before he thought better of it.

Freeman was as happy as he could be.

He was in his element.

As Skye reached for the supplies, Freeman offered to help.

"You have done far more than I could have imagined. I think I have it from here." Skye said, genuinely thankful.

"Is there anything I can do to repay you?" She continued.

"I do have some questions about your, eh, posture," Freeman said, unexpectedly fumbling.

Skye smiled, "Yes, it is an oddity."

"I'd be happy to tell you about it, do you have time later today," as she shifted the supplies to keep them balanced.

Freeman readily agreed, and they exchanged information.

Freeman spent the rest of his day running his route, bartering with vendors, and routing supplies back to the worksites.

Despite his curiosity and anticipation, every time he returned to the worksite, the nagging feeling that he wasn't getting any higher returned.

There had to be a better way.

CHAPTER 6: PROTOTYPE TEAM

Later on the day that Skye and Freeman first met; Freeman arrived at Skye's place of work. The inside was sparsely decorated and mostly disorganized.

For a moment, Freeman thought he might have the wrong place.

Then he heard noises above him.

"Hello?" Freeman called.

"Hi! I am up here!" Skye's voice called down from above.

While Bootsvillians have buildings with multiple floors, it is usually reserved for those who can afford it and for after work hours.

Being bent over, holding onto your bootstraps, presents a particular problem when going upstairs.

As Freeman stood hunched over in front of the stairs, he thought through his options.

The least desirable would be to lose his balance halfway up.

So, he decided to make a go at taking the stairs at full height, despite the cultural norms.

A soon as he stood, he was immediately plagued with doubt.

He was far from the etiquette of normal Bootsvillians.

But he comforted himself that Skye didn't appear to be "normal."

Seeing as he had limited choices, he climbed the stairs to see what Skye was doing.

Before he hit the top of the stairs, the smell of flowers greeted him, and something else; something that had to be freshly baked bread.

It's not that the smells were foreign to Freeman, but this entire experience had him off-kilter.

What in the world was she doing up there?

As he stepped out onto the second level, there were too many different inputs for him to process at once.

Freeman prepared himself to reassume the hunched over position, out of ingrained habit, but Skye had met him at the top of the stairs and put a cup into his hand before he had a chance to re-adjust.

Not that he could have re-adjusted quickly anyway, because the second floor wasn't enclosed as he thought.

It was open to the air.

But that wasn't entirely right.

Thick fabric was draped in layers, acting as solar shades.

There were various flowering and fruiting plants, as well as some herbs he couldn't quite identify.

There were different fixtures meant to catch the light and reflect it in patterns on the drapery.

There was a water fixture that quietly burbled.

And there was an outdoor oven with bread cooling on a rack.

Freeman had not seen any of this as he approached.

Even when Bootsvillians were not grabbing their bootstraps, many of them were perpetually canted forward, rarely looking up.

Freeman had not seen anything like this in Bootsville.

Freeman had never even heard of anything like this.

As he was trying to take all of it in, he realized that Skye was talking to him.

Rather that she had been talking to him and was now smiling at him.

"Who was this person?" he thought.

Quickly his people skills reasserted themselves.

"I am sorry, could you repeat that?" Freeman asked.

"I was asking you if you had found the place alright and thanking you again for your help today," Skye said with that same smile.

"But now I want to know what you think about my project?"

"After all, the supplies you helped me get today were instrumental in finishing it up," she continued.

"Well, I, uh… hmmm." Freeman stumbled, "Let me start again."

"This is amazing!"

"I have never seen anything like this."

"How long did it take you to do this?"

"When did you start?"

"Where did you get the idea?

"Who…"

Freeman rattled off questions in quick succession as he wandered across the rooftop.

Freeman's questions completely entertained Skye.

And she was unexpectedly energized by him having his eyes opened to something new.

"Which one of those do want me to answer first?" Skye asked, very caught up in the moment.

"Umm, how did you… no, umm, where did you… no… hmmm.

"I guess you need to start at the beginning and tell me everything." Freeman said, unable to find a landing place for his thoughts.

"Everything is a lot of things," Skye said playfully, "but it started a couple of months ago when I got fed up with my work."

Skye explained everything from her decision to stop trying to pull herself up by her bootstraps up until the time earlier that day when Freeman had helped her with Sal.

It took several hours, and while she was talking, Freeman would ask clarifying questions, but otherwise was paying rapt attention.

As she talked, they shared the fresh bread and several cups of tea.

And at the end of the story, Skye made an observation.

"The thing is, I have this vision for creating places that people can connect, share ideas, enjoy good company and conversations, and help each other. But do you know what I realized very clearly today?"

"What?" Freeman asked.

"I need people to help me." She stated matter of factly.

Skye let that statement hang out there.

She took a long drink of her tea and looked out over the darkening city.

It was at this moment she knew she was violating the cultural tenant of independence ingrained in Bootsvillians, and she wasn't sure how Freeman would react.

Caught up by Skye's vision of turning the canvas of Bootsville into a kaleidoscope of color and connections, her last comment came at Freeman like a cold splash of water to the face.

All that she had accomplished.

How she had spent almost all she had to make it a reality.

How she was just now beginning to realize the potential of her vision.

Her statement of need brought into stark reality the ways that she was different from the rest of the city.

What she was risking was more than just time and resources, she was risking becoming an outsider - and she was already beginning to experience that.

But what she was doing was much more significant than filing a supply route or moving up a little higher up in a pile.

It had meaning and purpose.

It was a higher calling that was so different from what the rest of the city was pursuing.

"Can I ask you a question?" Skye asked, breaking the silence.

"Absolutely," Freeman responded.

"Have you ever lifted yourself one inch higher by pulling on your bootstraps?"

Skye asked it plainly, though you could tell it was a question that she knew carried a tremendous amount of risk.

Freeman sat back, initially out of respect for Skye, who didn't seem to mind heaping one heresy upon another, but mostly because of the weight of the question.

"All that straining, day after day, have you ever succeeded in lifting yourself up?" She persisted.

Freeman's answer, as you already know, changed the course of his life.

Skye's vision resonated with him as it did with more after him, not everyone, but with those who were ready.

But this was the first time Skye found someone she instinctively knew was a person she needed to help complete the project.

"Freeman, what you did today with Sal... I would never have thought to do it, let alone pressed the way you did."

"You accomplished something that is not inside my strengths."

"Would you consider being a part of my team?"

Skye explained the concept of a team that was worked inside their strengths.

It was the first time she was trying to put her thoughts into words, and as Freeman and Skye's work continued, the explanation evolved and became more refined.

But for her first time saying it out loud, she did a pretty impressive job.

As Skye finished, Freeman sat forward.

Despite all of the cultural norms, despite the risk, Freeman said, "Yes."

And that night, on a rooftop inside the prototype of Skye's vision, a visionary and implementor set about the work of turning a vision into reality.

— — —

I wish I could report to you that they only experienced success from that point forward, but that is rarely the story.

Freeman let go of his bootstraps and, over the coming months, lost the callouses on his hands and began to straighten his posture.

Freeman kept many of his contacts but lost several of his best relationships due to the change.

He and Skye were able to cast the vision to other Bootsvillians.

Some caught it.

Skye's skills of casting the vision and Freeman's skills of implementing steps were a good match early on.

Still, as they had a couple of projects occurring at the same time, it became evident that Skye was no manager, and Freeman had a hard time telling which project took priority.

It created a strain that they committed to working through, but the longer it persisted, the more they both felt the burden of working outside their strengths.

After completing one project, which had gone in starts and stops, they came together to evaluate what was going on.

Was the vision good?
They agreed it was.

Was there work to be found?
Yes, if they could get out and communicate the vision.

Were they frivolous?
No, Freeman continued to get them good deals while maintaining healthy relationships.

So what were they lacking?
For all their skills, Skye and Freeman knew they were missing someone.
Between a visionary and an implementor, there needs to be an organizer.

And that is how they came about looking for Stanley Armstrong.

CHAPTER 7: NO

At the coffee table, over Stanley's break, Skye had just asked if she could ask Stanley a question.

In the moment that was about to happen, Freeman hope that Skye was able to work her magic.

Skye is far from being sorceress or magician, but as far as Freeman was concerned she had the same effect.

Skye is the kind of person that can make ideas seem like a reality, long before they ever take physical form.

She is a visionary.

She speaks in grand pictures and inspires people with a vision of what can be.

When she shares her vision with the right people, it can be like watching someone perform magic.

People entrenched in a dim view of the world, have a light come back into their eyes and are inspired to see the vision come to reality.

Freeman has his own set of skills, and as far as Skye was concerned, they were just as mystical.

Freeman is an implementor.

He has the skills to execute a plan and carry it out to the accomplishment of the objective.

Long after the casting of Skye's vision, Freeman is carrying it forward in practical ways.

How he can continue, day after day, to move in a direction, without distraction, is a mystery to Skye.

But in this moment, Freeman needed Skye to work her magic.

"Stanley, can I ask you a question?" Sky asked.

Stanley nodded affirmatively.

"Have you ever lifted yourself one inch higher by pulling on your bootstraps?" she asked and then continued, "By that, I mean, have you ever been able to lift yourself one inch off the ground by pulling on your bootstraps?"

Skye was meeting the directness of Stanley's questions ounce for ounce.

She wasn't trying to bait Stanley or patronize him into making a point.

She was asking him to take an honest look at himself.

Stanley sat back in his chair.

Up until now, he had been leaning forward, partly because of his posture but mostly because he was confident.

Not an intentional confidence per se, but a confidence born out of continued compliance and integration with the surrounding system.

Skye's question undercuts some of that confidence, and Stanley physically reacted to it by shifting in his seat.

Freeman and Skye both noticed the shift.

Both knew that what came next would be critical.

Stanley's brow furrowed, and he squinted his eyes.

It was a look of a man who was deep in thought and becoming deeply unsettled.

Stanley was unsettled.

Skye's question went against the primary doctrine of all good Bootsvillians.

Skye and Freeman had come to understand this through their previous conversation.

They know that a group of like-minded individuals who have coalesced into a community develops a tribe-like mentality.

Tribe-like mentalities are beneficial for those within the tribe.

They take care of each other, protect each other, speak a shared narrative, and have secure cultural touchstones.

But tribes are double-edged in that they can quickly identify who is "of" and "not of" the tribe.

Positively, dangerous individuals who pose a threat are quickly identified as being "not of" the tribe and can be dealt with to keep a tribe healthy.

Negatively, the tribe quickly identifies and can seek to deal with individuals who challenge stagnated cultural touchstones.

Skye and Freeman's posture was enough to make them stand out among other Bootsvillians.

Now adding to that, Skye was asking a question that sought to undercut the primary pillar of Bootsvillian culture.

This violation of cultural norms is why Skye and Freeman were watching Stanley intently.

They were aware that Stanley was now processing them as "not of" his tribe.

What they did not know is how he would react.

Skye was keenly aware of an "of" or "not of" reaction would happen even before she asked the question.

She, in an instant, made a calculated risk in being so direct.

She was aware that this could end negatively before it even began.

She was also aware that she risked immediate ostracization of her and Freeman by someone she saw as a prime candidate to round out their team.

She also knew that Freeman was well outside of his comfort zone.

Freeman was much less trusting of the unknown than Skye.

While Skye could effortlessly move into directions with no guaranteed outcome (and had - not always successfully), Freeman felt much better having clear, definable, and predictable objectives.

He trusted Skye, but at this moment, he was far outside of his strengths.

His relaxed position was becoming more and more alert.

And what was surely no more than a minute or two of silence started to stretch out before him.

Each second became more and more anxious for him.

He felt the need to step in and quell any possible adverse reaction from Stanley.

To steer Stanley through this question.

As it turns out, his intuition about Stanley's state of mind was accurate.

Stanley was dumbfounded at the question.

He heard what Skye said.

He even understood what Skye was asking.

But his mind could not seem to take hold of it in a meaningful way.

The question was foundational in that it seemed to be eroding his core beliefs.

But it also rang a bell in him, and that ringing could not be undone.

The sound was bouncing off the ingrained cultural pillars that were part of his very being.

It was discordant and disorienting.

After an unknown amount of time, he became aware that he had not responded to Skye, and both she and Freeman were staring at him.

Just as Freeman was reaching his limits and about to say something, Stanley broke his silence, "No."

One word.

Two letters.

But the meaning was miles wide.

Skye felt like a lightning bolt hit her, so much energy began to course through her.

But she knew what was happening in Stanley was not a celebration.

It was confusion.

Freeman, for his part, felt like he could melt.

His tension had become palpable, and that one-word answer let it release.

Sometimes these risks Skye would take were more than he thought he could bear.

Skye smiled, belying her genuine excitement, and gave a confirming reply, "No?"

"No," Stanley said again, but with no more confidence than the first time.

Honestly he felt a little ill.

Five minutes ago, his footing was sure.

Now, after one question, he felt like someone may be tipping the ground under him.

Skye just repeated gently, "No."

The pauses between the statements were just filled with quiet sips of their coffee, though Stanley left his untouched.

Freeman, having found his calm again, stepped in.

"Neither could we, Stanley."

"Not once in all of my pulling did I ever lift myself any higher than the ground or any person I could stand on."

"And do you know what Stanley?"

Stanley had been listening but had a thousand-yard-stare until Freeman brought his attention back to the moment.

He made eye contact with Freeman.

"I was unhappy, unsatisfied, and tired of not being able to get any higher."

"I knew there was a better way, but I couldn't see it."

Freeman's statement resonated with Stanley, deeply.

He was respected and good at his job, but at his core, he was frustrated.

Amid this swirl of thoughts and feelings, Stanley became aware of the time.

He knew that he had been away longer than anticipated and needed to get back to the pile.

There would be an oversupply of requests coming down from the top.

"I need to get back," Stanley said stoically.

Skye and Freeman understood, and as much as they wanted to continue the conversation, they didn't want to give Stanley too much too fast.

"Before you go," Skye added, "let me tell you, there is a better way."

"And we would very much like to talk to you more about what we are doing."

Skye and Freeman gave Stanley their contact information and asked him to contact them at a time when it would be good to talk.

Then Stanley left them and headed back to work, bootstraps in hand.

CHAPTER 8: STRAIN

That afternoon, after Stanley took his place in the pile, he could not settle back into his work.

As he looked down, the frustration of trying to organize the work rose inside him.

He found himself keenly aware of the weight of those above him.

He knew he was right about Skye and Freeman.

They were odd, and they had made him feel insecure.

But at the same time, they were the first people to speak out his deepest frustrations.

Was there a better way?

Stanley spent several days in a state of dis-ease.

That is to say, he was troubled.

His spirit had become disquieted, and he found that the daily grind was wearisome.

It would have been a stretch to say that he was ecstatic before meeting Skye and Freeman.

But he had been able to maintain steady footing if he didn't pay close attention to the why and how he did his job.

He just did it.

After all, he was a loyal Bootsvillian.

Hardworking.

Dedicated.

Independent.

But then there was Skye's question.

No, not just her question.

It was Skye and Freeman's whole demeanor, coupled with the question.

It had destabilized him.

They had destabilized him.

His first impression of them was correct.

These were not the kind of people with whom associating with was looked on favorably.

Stanley felt some assurance reassert itself.

He was carrying on the work of his father and his father's father.

It is just the way he did things.

He was a self-made man, picking himself up by his bootstraps.

But there was that question again, eroding at his core tenants.

"Have you ever lifted yourself one inch higher by pulling on your bootstraps?"

He had exerted exceptional effort and strain.

He was even hoping that he would have his own New Bootstrap Day sometime this next year.

After all, he had been pulling on his bootstraps very hard for a long time, and any day now they could snap.

This thought heartened Stanley for a moment, thinking of the celebration surrounding New Bootstrap Day, the recognition, the honor for his family.

But the feeling was very quick eroded by Skye's question and some of his own.

"What was he doing this all for?"

"A new set of bootstraps, so he could start pulling all over again?"

There was a rising discontent that Stanley could not ignore.

But he did not know how to deal with it, let alone who he could talk to about it.

He was worried that his family and co-workers would think him a complainer.

His choice about how many people he could discuss his thoughts with were very limited.

To be precise, there were only two.

CHAPTER 9: ANSWERS

Stanley's lack of response was not without concern for Skye and Freeman.

Both began to wonder if they needed to start looking elsewhere.

For Skye, who is not always able to tell how her intuition worked, Stanley felt like the right person.

He had the skill set, and she sensed that he had a spirit that was searching for a team.

For Freeman, this was all too unnerving.

There were too many uncontrollable variables.

Like Skye, he had believed that Stanley had the right skill set, and he appeared to have an underlying frustration, but Freeman was not prone to allowing things to play out without exerting control on them.

And this was precisely the reason Skye and Freeman were on a search for an organizer.

— — —

In the days since Stanley had talked to Skye and Freeman, Stanley began to feel like he had stomached about as much as he could.

His discontent was making him irritable with his family, the higher-ups, and those below him.

While it is infrequent for a Bootsvillian to take a day away from the job-site, Stanley decided he needed to put this to rest.

He let the higher-ups know that he would be out the next day and found a temporary replacement for himself.

That next morning he assumed the position and headed out to find Skye and Freeman.

But the further he went, the less and less confident he was.

He didn't know what he was looking to do or say.

He just knew he needed to find a way to resolve his internal conflict.

And since Skye and Freeman had been the ones who had agitated him, they were the best place to start looking for solutions.

Stanley arrived at the address Freeman had given him.

From the outside, it didn't look like much.

But as he stood at the door, he began to hear something, something that sounded like wind chimes.

And then a delightful smell wafted by him.

He looked to either side, but couldn't see from where it might be coming.

Trying to follow the sound, he looked up a high as he could.

If you have ever tried to lift your head and look high up at something, even if that something were normal, it might take a moment for your brain to process what you are seeing.

What Stanley saw was not normal and was not processing.

After several moments of confusion, he shook his head as if it might help him reconcile what he was seeing.

Coming over the side of the rooftop were green plants, with just a hint of color here and there.

A large piece of fabric or tarp was attached to a pole and stretched beyond his sight.

The sound of the chimes was persistent and quite charming.

And the smell that wafted down from made his mouth water.

He felt inexorably drawn to the roof.

He wanted to see more than just this very acute angle.

Knocking on the door, he was greeted by a muffled, "Come in!"

Taking the invitation, he stepped across the threshold to find himself in a room that, if he was generous, was disorganized.

If he wasn't generous, it was chaos.

The wall was busy with papers, drawings, maps, and hastily written notes on small pieces of paper taped to it.

His disdain for the disorder almost entirely supplanted the draw that he felt outside.

Doubt reasserted itself on a very personal level.

Stanley, thankfully, was not given much time by himself in the room, as Sky and Freeman came down a set of stairs together.

They both made no effort to hide their happiness at seeing him.

"Stanley! I am so glad you came!" said Skye as she quickened her pace.

Her demeanor was genuine and warm.

"Yes, yes, it is good to see you," said Freeman.

Freeman's demeanor, while as warm as Skye's, was tinged with a sense of relief.

Reaching to greet them both, Stanley said, "Uh, thank you. I uh... well, I guess it was time for me to talk about the specifics of what it is you are doing."

Usually very articulate, Stanley felt a bit thrown by his experience outside and the environment around him.

Skye, caught up in her happiness and ignoring his awkwardness, answered first, "Absolutely! I am just so glad you decide to come."

"Please, come with us."

Skye and Freeman led Stanley up the stairs to the roof.

And as much as the room below agitated Stanley, his curiosity about what lay above began to assert itself.

This experience was turning into a bit of a rollercoaster of competing emotions for him.

Skye and Freeman said very little as they ascended the stairs, but at the top, Skye turned to him with a barely concealed smile and said, "It would be easier to show you what we are doing."

I wish it were easier to convey to you the sensory overload that Stanley experienced, but so much hit him at once that he felt like he was having an out of body experience.

The smell was the first thing to hit him.

Strong, earthy, with hints of sweet floral, and a base of baking bread.

But the next thing that registered were the sounds.

Chimes moving in a gentle breeze.

Metallic and sweet from one direction, and wooden and resonate from another.

And a faint undertone of burbling water.

As he stepped out onto the rooftop, he took a minute to survey the entire environment.

Flowering plants mixed with fruit and vegetable bearing plants were making a vibrant hue of colors against the green.

Solar shades were blocking most, but not all, of the light, causing the light to play across the wooden and tiled flooring.

A water fixture that splashed water down several rocks, weaving in and out the light and casting reflections back up on the solar shades.

A stone oven filled with several loaves of bread.

High seats were around a table in one corner, and low chairs were in the center around an unlit fire pit.

A journal lay on the corner table, where someone had been sitting and drinking a cup of tea.

The glass of tea and pitcher both had small beads of water condensed and slowly rolling down their sides.

Steadying himself with his hand against the back of a chair, Stanley closed his eyes and allowed it to wash over him.

A deep and abiding sense of calm began displacing the doubt and anxiety.

And at that moment, Stanley just was.

There was no frustration from what had happened or needed to happen at the pile; no anxiety about what he was doing here with Skye and Freeman.

Stanley, for a few precious moments, just existed at peace.

He did not know how long he stood there like that.

Time starts to loosen its grasp in a place of peace.

But eventually, he remembered that he was not alone and opened his eyes.

Skye and Freeman had taken seats equidistance from him around the fire pit.

Skye had picked up her journal and was writing in it.

Freeman had picked up a glass of tea and was casually sipping it as he sat quietly.

Seeing Stanley stir, they both looked at him and smiled brightly and knowingly.

"Stanley, please, have a seat," said Freeman as he motioned to the seat Stanley had been steadying himself on.

Feeling somewhat sheepish, Stanley nodded and took it.

As he sat, he noticed the cup of tea poured for him.

Skye closed her journal and folded her hands over the top of her legs.

"This is what we are doing," she said.

"Creating micro-ecosystems for individuals to foster and share life with others."

Her pride was evident, but not off-putting.

As Stanley nursed his tea, Skye told him of her journey and vision to create a living mural of micro-ecosystem across the city.

Freeman interjected as needed, to help flesh out details.

And as Skye wound down, Freeman shared his story and what drew him to join Skye.

While Freeman was talking, he poured Stanley another cup of tea, and Skye pulled out the bread that had been baking to let it cool.

She opened yet another door and began cutting fruit, vegetables, and cheese.

Skye added to Freeman's story in the same manner as he had to hers.

As Freeman finished, Skye had brought back individual wooden platters with a hunk of bread, slices of white cheese, and cut fruits and vegetables of various kinds.

Stanley had listened attentively to both of their stories and had felt no need to ask questions.

They sat in silence for a few moments as they each ate from their platter.

During their meal, Stanley paused and looked around, taking in again the scope of what Skye and Freeman had built.

"Not in my wildest imagination could I have come up with what you have done here."

"It is so beautiful, peaceful, and ambitious," he said with a sincerity that surprised himself.

"But," doubt creeping back into his voice, "what can I offer to something like this?"

"I have spent my career in the middle of the pile."

"Sending down orders for supplies and passing those supplies up to the top."

"I don't know that I have much to offer you." he reiterated, now with a touch of sadness.

In the time that had passed from leaving the house to this mid-day meal, something had happened to Stanley.

What seemed possible this morning was small compared to what he was experiencing.

The story and reality of what Skye and Freeman were doing resonated deep inside of Stanley's being.

The sadness he felt was the result of knowing that a bell was ringing inside him that could not be un-rung.

He began to doubt that he had anything to offer these people on their journey.

And what he was going back to was never going to inspire him as he had been today.

Skye's and Freeman became serious as they took in what Stanley was saying.

And with deep authority and respect, Skye said, "Stanley, I know you have been stepped on your entire career."

"I know that this city says that if we just pull hard enough on our bootstraps that we will lift ourselves higher."

"But the truth is, the only way anyone in this city has gotten higher is by stepping on others."

She allowed what she said to hang in the air for a moment and sink in.

"What we are creating is not being done by stepping on anyone else."

"What we are creating is being done by letting go of the way we had been doing it our entire lives."

"By extending to our full height, focusing on what we are good at, and being open and agile enough to identify and take advantage of unique opportunities."

"What you are sitting in exists because we took our eyes off the ground and looked around at what could be."

"But what you are sitting in is only one of a few places we have been able to create."

"We are struggling to effectively organize our resources to create more unique micro-ecosystems in the city."

"Stanley, we have already told you that Skye can envision that which doesn't exist yet and that I have full confidence in my ability to find and deliver on a defined project," Freeman added.

"But neither of us can organize Skye's vision into actionable, source-able, steps that can be replicated and delivered consistently and sustainably."

"We need someone who can organize this initiative."

"And we believe that person is you." Freeman finished with directness.

"We teeter on the point of failure," said Skye.

"Failure by not being able to accomplish a vision that is bigger than either one of us."

"We know that for us to succeed, we need someone who has skills and abilities we don't possess."

"And as Freeman said, we believe that someone is you."

"I mean, have you seen our project room," she said with a wry smile.

"Would you join us, Stanley, and bring your skills to our team?" Skye finished with transparency and vulnerability.

"I saw the room," said Stanley, suppressing a shudder.

"And I hear what you are saying."

"Though I am not sure where your confidence in me comes from, I am humbled by it."

He paused for a moment.

"What is your timeline?"

"How soon do you need to know if I would like to join you?"

"The sooner, the better," said Freeman.

"We had hoped to be further along than we are now, but our disorganization has held us back."

"And if you are to pass on this, we need to find someone else or risk total failure."

"That is an... unappealing potential outcome."

"We have invested a significant amount of time and resources in the initiative already, and we truly believe it will do good for this city."

"Could you have us an answer within the week?" Freeman asked.

Stanley thought for a moment and agreed that he could.

As he stood to leave, he took one more look around the roof, trying to memorize this experience, in case it was his last.

He thanked them both and head back down and out of the building.

Skye and Freeman walked him out and thanked him for coming.

As Stanley walked down the street, he heard the door close behind him.

After he was about a block away, he turned around and looked at the building.

There he saw Skye and Freeman moving and talking with one another.

He saw the splash of color from the plants and colored shades, and he thought he could barely make out the sound of the chimes.

At that moment, he became keenly aware that he was standing at full height in the middle of the road as other Bootsvillians shuffled around him.

Instinctually he began to reach for his bootstraps.

Then the sound of the chimes came through clearly in a brief lull in the sounds of the city

He looked back up, stood up straight, and for the first time, walked home standing at full height.

Chapter 10: Breaking Point

The next day Stanley got ready to head back to the pile.

Despite the walk back from his meeting with Skye and Freeman the day before, he still found himself assuming the position on his way to work.

As he arrived at the pile, the discontentment, lurking around the edges of his mind, came to full reality as he stepped upon the lifters and took his place midway up the pile.

The shifting under his feet made him feel uneasy for the first time.

He felt the weight of those above him, and it felt the heaviest it ever had.

He decided that he would grin and bear it and deal with the discontentment later.

At the moment he decided to accept his place in the pile, Stanley felt a snap at both of his heels.

Two snaps in quick succession, which resulted in him jerking upward unexpectedly.

He caught himself before flying up to full height, but his sudden movement sent a ripple through the pile.

As the startled utterances from above died down, Stanley made the necessary apologies.

Then he looked at his hands.

Between both his thumbs and forefingers, he held the torn bootstraps from his boots.

He felt the back of his boots to be sure.

Sure enough, he had succeeded in tearing off both of his bootstraps at the same time.

His colleagues in the pile noticed the disturbance and his weird behavior.

Then they saw his hands.

What started as a whisper of awe rose into a cacophony of voices and shouts.

Stanley had never broken a bootstrap before.

And while he had been around when others had broken a bootstrap, he had never seen someone break two.

The shouts turned into celebratory back slaps and congratulations from all up and down the pile.

The higher-ups even came down to congratulate him and marvel at the accomplishment.

They were sure this meant that he was supposed to be higher up in the pile someday.

Such a rare feat of strength had to mean Stanley was designed for a higher purpose.

The boss of the pile even had a replacement called up and called Stanley out to make a poignant speech about the rewards of being hardworking, dedicated, and independent.

The boss then presented Stanley with an award of two brand-new bootstraps paid for by the company and going so far as to refer him to his cobbler, so that Stanley would receive the best treatment.

The boss then gave Stanley the rest of the day off to get his new bootstraps so he could come back the next day to show them off.

Everyone cheered, and it was a very boisterous celebration.

Even folks from nearby piles came by to see what was happening.

But as Stanley stood there, with his bootstraps in his hands, the celebration seemed to happen around him.

He kindly thanked people and smiled at the congratulations.

He even stopped for a couple of pictures.

But in a moment that is a massive accomplishment for a Bootsvillian, he felt the emptiness of futility.

Skye's words filled his head.

In this fog, he moved on auto-pilot.

He was going through the motions, with the celebrants shrugging off his silence as him being overwhelmed.

He was overwhelmed, just not like he thought he should be.

He took the boss up on his recommendation to us the cobbler, and Stanely made his way, bootstraps in hand, to the store.

The cobbler was waiting for him.

The boss had already called ahead and told him that Stanley was coming.

Everyone in the shop started another round of celebratory remarks.

Stanley was gracious, but he felt like he was hiding behind a mask.

The shopkeeper said that he has only seen this happen a handful of times, and he is sure that people will be talking about it for years.

No one could doubt Stanley's ability to be a hardworking, dedicated, and independent Bootsvillian.

"Nope... nobody could doubt it." thought Stanley to himself.

As he took a chair to wait for the cobbler to begin his work, he felt himself sink deeper into his melancholy.

"What is wrong with me?" he kept thinking to himself.

"This should be a day, unlike any other day."

As these thoughts dragged his spirit down, he was vaguely aware that another customer had come into the shop.

As he sat and stewed, he overheard part of the conversation that dragged him out of his inner monologue.

Looking up, he saw a Bootsvillian who had come in to pick up an order of new boots.

He had a badge on his sleeve that had the initials BDE.

Bootsville Department of Energy.

The cobbler seemed to know this individual, as they had a very natural conversation.

The government worker was anxious about something.

As the BDE employee talked, he told the cobbler that the BDE was trying everything it could to amplify the supply of energy to the city, but that they were at severe risk of having to implement rolling blackouts in the next six months if this continued.

The city was using too much energy.

The energy supply was insufficient to meet demands.

And the energy network was overtaxed and in need of an upgrade.

He told the cobbler that they should prepare if a solution did not present itself soon.

After several more minutes of concerned conversation, the worker left the shop with his new pair of shoes.

This threat to the city sidelined Stanley's issues.

Rolling blackouts would mean losses across the city.

Food would not store reliably.

Businesses would lose productivity, potentially leading to lost jobs.

Constructions projects would grind to a halt for undefined periods.

The potential for chaos layout in front of Stanley as if it were happening.

Stanley, not knowing why, stood up.

Feeling a call to action and need to do something for his community, his city.

But what?

What could he do?

He didn't know how to make more energy for the city.

He had no idea how to fix this problem.

He stood at the window of the shop and looked out across the street.

He looked at all of the people shuffling about their day to day business.

Then he looked up.

He saw the plainness of the rooftops, and an idea struck him, not a solution, but maybe a way to a solution.

He took off out of the shop with the cobbler calling after him.

He was going to find Skye and Freeman.

If they could create something as unexpected as the garden he encountered, maybe they could find a solution.

Stanley was so focused that he didn't realize that he left his bootstraps on the cobbler's counter.

CHAPTER 11: INSPIRATION

A short time later, Stanley rushed up to the building that Skye and Freeman used as their office and prototype.

His mind was turning the problem over as he made his way there, but he felt no closer to a solution.

Skye and Freeman greeted him with excitement and welcomed him in.

For their part, seeing him again so soon had to be a positive sign.

But they were unprepared for the reality of the situation.

They didn't have time for tea and freshly made bread today.

Stanley barely made it through the door before he began to tell them what he had just overheard at the cobbler's shop.

As the three of them stood in the cluttered office, Stanley relayed to Skye and Freeman what had happened that day at the pile, what he had overheard the cobbler's, and what he saw the ramifications being if the energy crisis came to pass.

Where the room had before created anxiety for Stanley, it now seemed to create a safe space for him to share without reservation.

With unexpected transparency, he shared not just the events of the day, but also how hollow it all had felt.

Skye and Freeman listened intently, feeling the weight of the situation.

A mix of emotions ran through them, hearing about the tearing of the bootstraps, the celebration, and the news of the imminent energy crisis.

Stanley's transparency was moving, but at the same time, not the focal point of the moment.

"I just felt this overwhelming need to do something."

"And the only thing I could think of was that you two, of anyone I know, could come up with a solution."

"And that if you will have me, I want to be part of delivering that solution." Stanley finished, feeling spent.

He reached out to lean on the back of a chair and found himself just sitting down.

He felt vulnerable, drained, and a bit anxious at the thought that he might be acting foolishly.

"First, welcome aboard," Freeman said as he reached out a reassuring hand.

"Second, are you sure?" he said with a concerned expression.

"I only know what I heard, and the level of concern appeared to be genuine." Stanley reiterated.

"You're right." Freeman agreed.

"If this energy crisis comes to pass, then the city would be challenged and changed... and what we are doing here would be the last thing anyone would be thinking about." Freeman said with a worried tone as he too sat down in an empty chair.

Skye was taking this in, but she could not sit down.

She began pacing, only partially aware that Stanley and Freeman had gone silent.

Her mind spun up its creative engine faster and faster, first surrounding the problem to try and understand it, then lashing out in multiple directions at once to find a solution.

Amid this brainstorming, she heard the wind chimes from the roof above her.

She stopped and listened.

Then like a bolt of lightning arcing from point to point almost quicker than the eye can see, the full solution presented itself.

She took off up the stairs, knowing that if she did not capture this moment, she would soon lose grasp of it.

So sudden was her movement that Stanley started up out of his chair looking concerned.

Freeman put up his hand and said, "She'll be back."

And with a half-smile added, "Something has come to her—we'll just have to wait for her to share it with us."

As Freeman retrieved refreshments for him and Stanley, and they examined and re-examined the problem for multiple angles, Skye had grabbed her journal and started to write in broken sentences and sketching shapes and images that were half-formed.

With a surge of creativity fueling her, she tried to capture the fullness of the ideas that were cascading over her.

And as the flow gratefully began to slow, she was able to go back over what she had written and drawn.

Starting again to try and make sense of it, she outlined and tried to flesh out some of the designs.

After what seemed like only moments to her, she heard Freeman talking to her.

"So. What did you come up with?" Freeman asked.

Skye looked back to see that the afternoon had passed into early evening and that Freeman was holding out a drink and platter of food to her.

Stanley was seated by the fire pit and looked more at ease.

Skye gladly took the platter and cup and tucked her journal under her arm.

She joined Freeman and Stanley around the fire.

After taking a moment to drink, eat, and gaze into the fire, she felt that she had gathered her thoughts enough to share them.

Throughout the evening, their conversation went up and down many paths.

But Skye's idea can be succinctly stated.

Her wide-ranging curiosity had always driven her to consume information from random and disparate sources.

Several of those sources dealt with wind and solar energy generation that was used by some of the farming settlements outside the central energy infrastructure of the city.

Skye's idea was to take and modify those methods of generation to weave the ability to generate supplemental energy into the micro-ecosystems they designed.

She showed Freeman and Stanley her sketches for low profile designs that could capture the wind and solar energy like the chimes and solar shades already were.

There were many, many questions from Stanley and Freeman.

Not all of which were answerable by Skye.

But as they talked, the concept became more and more sound.

As the night drew in, they all sat feeling mentally strained but oddly energized by everything they had discussed.

Skye had shared, answered, and redesigned to the point that she was sitting silently, just letting the flame transfix her mind for a time.

Eventually she said something that had become a maxim of sorts for her, "Decisions are made. Problems are solved."

She let it hang there in the air for a moment, then added, "I want to do this."

"Are we in agreement?" she asked with respect and authority.

Freeman knew Skye well enough to know that if he said yes, that they were committing themselves to a course of action.

And he felt like this idea had legs, and that he could be those legs in delivering on it.

He also felt a twinge of excitement as he looked to Stanley and said, "Well, Stan, I am in if you can tell me how we do it."

For their new team, this was the first time they would be leaning into Stanley's strengths of organization and problem-solving.

Stanley felt like Skye had set loose an avalanche of possibility.

Though through the course of the evening, he believed he had a grip on what needed to happen.

Looking to Freeman, Stanley first said, "Stan... nobody's ever called me that before. I kind of like it."

Then he said, "I say let's do it."

The power of their agreement was tangible.

Stan used that energy to outline his thoughts on what the project would entail, what information they needed to know, what resources would be required, and what kind of people they would need to talk to so that they could deliver this idea.

While the three of them worked to flesh out Skye's vision, it was largely Freeman and Stan who added the details.

Skye's part in the conversation was adding potential connections and thinking through possible solutions when they would run into roadblocks.

They worked long into the night until the initial burst of energy began to wear off, and the length of the day began to settle on them.

They adjourned, agreeing to do some individual work the next morning and making plans to get together again after lunch the next day.

The decision made, they now were searching out solutions to the problems that presented themselves.

CHAPTER 12: SKYE, FREEMAN, AND STAN

The length, breadth, and depth of their journey from concept to reality was detailed and nuanced.

Stan tendered his resignation, much to the surprise of the higher-ups at his pile.

He gave up the standard Bootsvillian posture in exchange for the more agile upright stance.

He did retrieve his bootstraps from the Cobbler's shop, as he found that the story of the dual bootstrap tear, while meaningless to him now, did open doors and create opportunities to talk to the people they needed to get in front of.

Focus and meaning replaced the nagging doubt.

His family did the best they could to support him, though it took them time to understand what exactly he was doing.

But eventually, they started to come around as well.

Freeman leveraged all of his contacts, and developed a few new ones, to find what they needed to build prototypes at a few micro-ecosystems that they already had made.

Working with Skye had always been exciting, but Stan's precision and attention to detail gave him peace of mind that he could deliver on what was needed when it was needed.

He saw the path they needed to take and knew what he needed to do next.

He even found himself better able to judge how much he needed to haggle and spend to make sure they had enough for the entire project.

He was in a happy place.

Skye was too.

In all the projects before this one, she felt the need to understand and carry forward every detail.

And she had always felt inadequate to the task.

It took a tremendous amount of energy and effort for her to try and operate in the space that Stan seemed to move in effortlessly.

And she found herself able to focus on what she was best at—brainstorming solutions to the problems they encountered and inspiring people with the vision of what they were trying to accomplish.

With Stan's strengths and skills, they were able to accomplish more in a month than they had in half a year.

The first month of their work together as a team was not without struggles and setbacks.

But each of them trusted and relied on each other to focus on what they did best.

The result, problem upon problem was solved and, within a relatively short amount of time, they had several working prototypes in operation at their rooftop micro-ecosystems.

Their vision was being made a reality through Skye's creativity, Stan's organization, and Freeman's resourcing.

As they prepared to switch on the power input from the prototype to the building power supply, they were giddy and anxious.

Freeman smiled at Stan, Skye, and the team they had built and reached for the switch.

"All of you, this project is a success because of you." He beamed as he spoke.

And, if it isn't too passé, let there be light!"

As Freeman flipped the switch to allow power from the prototypes to feed into the building, the lights dimmed for just an instant and then came back to full strength.

The meter that tracked how much energy the building consumed slowed down until it was moving at a leisurely pace.

They had managed to replace almost half the energy usage of the building with their alternative energy sources.

A cheer went up amongst the team!

There was a good deal of celebration and more than a few tears of joy.

This team had taken the concept of a micro-ecosystem and evolved it to reduce the amount of energy it took to run a modest-sized building.

Through a combination of flexible solar panels woven into the solar shades and cylindrical and tear shape wind turbines, they had harnessed the natural energy already present in the city.

And now they knew they had a solution to a looming crisis for Bootsville.

Their next challenge was to bring this to the decision-makers.

As hard as the process was to create a working solution, the challenge of getting buy-in from bureaucrats loomed darkly in front of them.

CHAPTER 13: THE HEAD MAN

During the development of the project, the looming energy crisis had become public.

Anxiety was high, and solutions were few.

What solutions were present were going to be onerous.

Planned cutbacks in operations.

Rolling brownouts.

Enforcement of energy reduction laws across the city.

It was into this environment that the energy generating component of the micro-ecosystems was trying to gain a foothold.

And fortunately for Skye and Freeman, Stan's prior success in the pile had given him a modicum of respect across the city.

The story of the mid-level manager that broke both his bootstraps had made rounds through even the highest level Bootsvillian bureaucracy.

You should take note that Bootsvillian bureaucrats are renowned for their inflexibility and general lack of creativity.

They firmly believe that everything and everyone has a place and they should stay in it.

This belief depresses a significant amount of creativity and innovation.

Their inflexibility, combined with the constant downward-facing trajectory of Bootsvillians, led to the austerity measures that were in preparation for implementation.

Stan leveraged his story wherever he could to gain access to the head of the Bootsville Department of Energy.

The head man's office was austere and decorated with his awards and certifications.

On his desk, he had a glass-backed picture frame that showed a torn bootstrap.

As Stan, Skye, and Freeman entered the head man looked up with a not-unpleasant expression and welcomed them to his office.

They exchanged rudimentary pleasantries, and, as with most Bootsvillians, the head man asked after Stan's story with some eagerness.

Stan had, by this time, told his story more than a few times.

He had learned what to focus on, and what leave out, to avoid being drawn into a lengthy discussion of his new style of work.

Without embellishment, Stan relayed the occurrences of the day and produced the broken straps for the head man to see.

And as had become normal among listeners of Stan's story, the headman was transfixed by the sight of the actual bootstraps.

So strong was his belief that the broken bootstraps were a sign of success that he became misty-eyed.

Stan allowed the moment to be still, out of respect for the head man.

There is no doubt that Skye was indeed the visionary of the project.

And when it came to inspiring people, she was the one who did most of the talking.

But this environment was less about inspiring, and more about convincing.

Skye's attention waned when the conversation turned to the practicalities of delivery on their vision.

But Stan's attention became laser-focused.

As much as Stan believed in the whole vision of the rooftop micro-ecosystems and their potential impact on individual and community wellbeing, he knew that the following presentation needed to focus on their ability to impact the coming energy crisis.

After patiently answering questions from the head man about the bootstraps, Stan took the opportunity to explain the reason behind the meeting.

Over what seemed to be a small eternity to Skye, Stan explained the energy portion of their project, what they had accomplished, and, with far more numbers than Skye was interested in absorbing, he explained what the project could achieve if deployed across 10%, 20%, and 30% of the city.

As Stan spoke, Freeman interspersed information about resource availability, logistics, and costs of deployment across regions of the city.

The headman listened carefully, asking only a few questions.

His face was unreadable, and it was making Skye uncomfortable.

She knew that Stan was giving the head man what was needed to convince him of the feasibility of their project, but she wanted him to be inspired too.

If only she knew how hard it was to inspire intransigent bureaucracy, she might not have been so eager.

As Freeman finished his portion of the presentation, a silence settled on the office.

Stan and Freeman felt energized but uncertain.

Skye felt like she was going to vomit—either words or the content of her stomach; she wasn't sure which yet.

Thankfully, after a few seconds, the headman spoke.

"I want to see it," he said.

All three of them felt a palpable release of tension.

Stan smiled and made arrangements with the headman, and his team, to come by the next day.

They all three thanked him and left the office.

While they were far from certain that the city would get behind the project, they felt almost as giddy as when they had turned on the power generation the first time.

— — —

The next day the headman and his team shuffled down the street towards the prototype project.

Skye saw them coming from the rooftop and rushed down to meet them.

She had spent the morning ruminating over the details of the rooftop.

Clipping and shaping the plants.

Kneading bread dough and setting it to rise.

Having Stan and Freeman help with general cleaning, when they weren't pouring over their numbers in preparation for questions.

The last half hour before the meeting had been hardest on Skye.

She had done her part, and now she just had to wait.

Skye was not a creature of stillness, especially when an opportunity was preparing to birth.

But she forced herself just to breathe and take in the beauty of the environment.

She was marginally successful, at least enough so that Stan and Freeman were able to finish their preparation in relative peace.

As she rushed to the door to welcome the headman and his team, her smile and enthusiasm were genuine.

She welcomed them to the building and showed them upstairs.

As they passed through the downstairs room, Stan's influence was already evident; he had organized the lower room into an immaculate model of efficiency.

The order and organization created a sense of peace that Skye found comforting—even if at times she continued to be an agent of chaos in that order.

As the headman and his team entered the rooftop space, they each gave a reaction that was immensely satisfying to Skye.

As each traversed to a different feature of the space, smiles spread across their faces.

The headman, for his part, found himself drawn to the burbling water feature.

Skye, with great enthusiasm and flair, talked about each part of the eco-system and explained how it helped to create the whole environment.

Each listened as they explored.

Freeman sidled up to several to have more intimate conversations regarding specific aspects of the space and only excused himself to pull the freshly baked bread from the stone oven.

The presence of the bread was almost enough to overshadow Skye's explanation.

As Skye wound down her explanation, she nodded to Stan.

Stan invited the headman and his team to come over to a monitor and switch they had mounted on the roof for the demonstration.

Stan explained the ways solar and wind energy were being captured and showed how it interconnected with the Bootsvillian energy network.

He answered several questions from the team, as Freeman passed out information sheets.

He then invited the head man to flip the switch allowing the energy to flow into the building.

As the head man flipped the switch, all eyes were on the display that was showing the real-time amount of energy the building was consuming.

There were several excited murmurs as the meter slowed to half its rate of consumption and held steady.

More questions started to come at Stan and Freeman, and they quickly divided up the organizational issues to Stan and logistical problems to Freeman.

They talked for well over an hour, moving from positions around the monitor to sitting around the rooftop soaking up the environment, partaking in the bread, and sipping on tea.

As the discussion continued, Skye noticed the headman slip back to the water installation.

At first, she respected his space while he studied the fixture, but after a few minutes, she silently joined him as the conversation continued behind them.

After some time, the headman said, "So you are responsible for this?"

"It was a team effort," Skye replied with pride and an inescapable smile.

Not taking his eyes off the water, he said, "I had no idea anything like this was happening in the city."

"There is a calmness here," he continued quietly.

"When you combine that with the energy it is capturing, it gives me a deep sense of peace and hope." His voice trailed off contently.

Skye smiled and let the stillness linger.

Then she said, "It is my, I mean, our hope that we can create these spaces across the city and bring this same sense of purpose, peace, and hope to as many people as possible."

"I can see that being a good thing," the head man said as he looked at Skye, "and you have my support to make it happen."

A smile so big it made her cheeks hurt took over Skye's face, but she understood the weight and honor of what he said too.

Making only the smallest effort to suppress the smile, but allowing her eyes to communicate the sincerity of her gratitude, she thanked him for his support with depth and resonance.

He nodded to her and stepped over to his team.

Cutting into the discussion, he told them of his decision to support this initiative and help resource the energy capture portion of it, while leaving the creative aspect to Skye, Stan, and Freeman to work out as they best see fit across the city.

There were nods all around and congratulations to Skye, Stan, and Freeman by the head man and his team.

While no project leaps into action at the moment of decision, the head man's support opened doors and created access to resources that made creating new locations incentivizing for building owners.

And as the wheels set into motion, unique micro-ecosystems began to pop up all over the city.

The addition of energy to the network was small at first, but as more and more sites began to go online, the strain on the city's resources began to lessen.

Energy-saving measures where implemented, but they were less austere than had been anticipated.

Anxiety dropped across the city, and people were actively seeking out Skye, Stan, and Freeman to come and design the rooftop micro-ecosystems for them.

More than that, people began giving credibility to this new work style that the team was modeling.

Not everyone let go of their bootstraps to seek out new opportunities, but for those that were willing to Skye, Stan, and Freeman were there to support them through the uncertainty.

Their team grew to meet demand, and they were meticulous in putting people in positions that matched their skill set.

And as their success grew, so did their legacy.

CHAPTER 14: EPILOGUE

Those hard-working, dedicated, and independent Bootsvillians became smarter in how they worked hard, stretched their dedication to encompassing a vision that was larger than their limited sight, and traded in the isolation of their independence for the support of teams that believe in them.

As you look at Bootsville now, you will notice that not everyone hunches over, shuffling about their jobs.

You will see what was once just a functional and bland cityscape blooming with color and innovation, one rooftop at a time.

And if you look closely, you will see a trio of people making a difference in their community.

As for Stan, his change was never fully understood by everyone around him, but he wasn't concerned about their approval anymore.

He was far more concerned about what he could do to make a difference and improve himself, his team, and his community.

Over the years, his back straightened as much as his spirit had.

He belonged to a team that valued him and what he was good at, and he appreciated them for everything they brought to the table.

As the vision continued to grow and change, he was there to meet the changes with new solutions and processes.

Skye and Freeman trusted him implicitly as he would interpret the vision and provide clearly defined plans for implementation.

And far from the piles where Bootsvillians were still stepping on each other to get higher up, they were lifting each other to heights they could never have reached on their own.

THE END

ABOUT THE AUTHOR

Chris is the Managing Partner and sole of owner of White Law Office, Co. His ideas on team building are influenced by experience and real time application of the principals found in "Bootsville."

Based on those principals, Chris and his team grew a single office rural practice into a multimillion dollar regional client-focused legal service provider.

When he isn't leading his team at White Law Office, Co., you might find him hanging out with his family, waiting on ballet practice to end, speaking, teaching, directing, writing, brainstorming, gaming, or playing tabletop role playing games with players around the world.

Thank you for reading "Bootsville"!

CMW

Christopher M. White

j3eight, ltd – j3eight.com